YOUR KNOWLEDGE HAS VALUE

Rolf Tanner

Middle East Enigma. Managing Political and Economic Risks on the Ground

A Hundred Years War

GRIN Publishing

Bibliographic information published by the German National Library:

The German National Library lists this publication in the National Bibliography; detailed bibliographic data are available on the Internet at http://dnb.dnb.de .

Imprint:

Copyright © 2015 GRIN Verlag GmbH
Print and binding: Books on Demand GmbH, Norderstedt Germany
ISBN: 978-3-656-97107-8

This book at GRIN:

http://www.grin.com/en/e-book/295676/middle-east-enigma-managing-political-and-economic-risks-on-the-ground

GRIN - Your knowledge has value

Since its foundation in 1998, GRIN has specialized in publishing academic texts by students, college teachers and other academics as e-book and printed book. The website www.grin.com is an ideal platform for presenting term papers, final papers, scientific essays, dissertations and specialist books.

Visit us on the internet:

http://www.grin.com/

http://www.facebook.com/grincom

http://www.twitter.com/grin_com

"Middle East Enigma: Managing Political and Economic Risks on the Ground – A Hundred Years' War."

Dr. Rolf Tanner, polecor

Good evening, ladies and gentlemen.

I would like to open my presentation tonight with a little fable. The fable was told to me about 20 years ago by Dr. Michael Burrell, then a Middle East scholar at the London School of Oriental and African Studies (SOAS), on the occasion of some commiserating about the seeming fact that spoilers apparently always have the upper hand in the region when it comes to the matters of peace and war.

The fable goes as following:

A frog and a scorpion want to cross the Suez Canal. For the frog, this of course isn't a problem as he knows how to swim. For the scorpion, however, this is a problem because he doesn't know how to swim. So he asks the frog: "Can you give me a lift, buddy? I need to get to the other side." The frog shirks and says: "Why should I do that? You are a malicious animal, and you are going to sting me as soon as you are on my back." The scorpion responds: "Come on, why should I do that? It would be really stupid because when I am stinging you while swimming, we are both going to drown." The frog thinks for a moment: 'Mmmh, that's true. Why should he do that?' So he turns around and says to the scorpion:"OK, fine, get on my back, I bring you to the other side." The scorpion crawls on the back of the frog, the frog gets into the water and starts swimming. But when they are in the middle of the Suez Canal, the scorpion stings the frog. The frog, knowing he is going to die, turns around and asks with his last breath before drowning: "WHY have you done this??" The scorpion only responds: "Remember – we are in the Middle East!"

A story of irrational behaviour and senseless violence. And unfortunately, when we listen to the news coming out of the Middle East on an almost daily basis, we are very often confronted with such senseless violence and completely irrational behaviour.

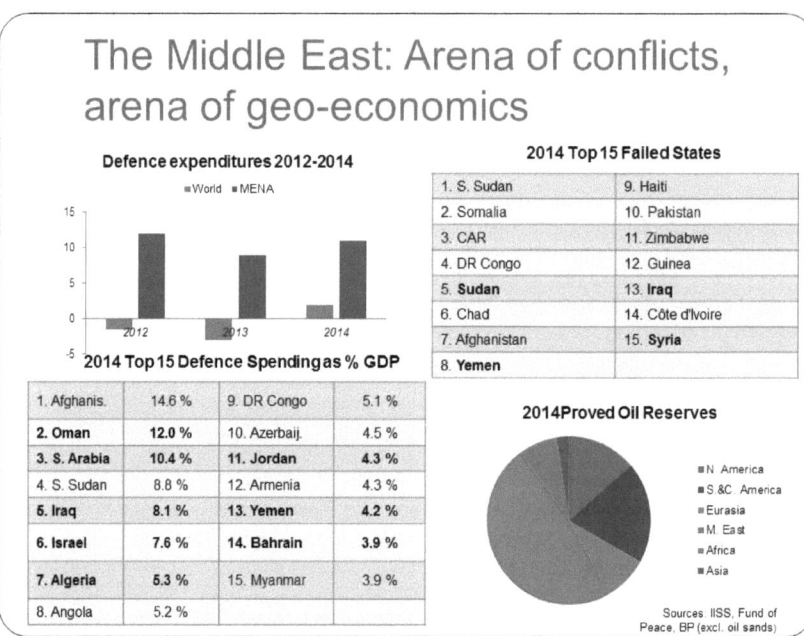

The Middle East: Arena of conflicts, arena of geo-economics

Defence expenditures 2012-2014

■World ■MENA

2014 Top 15 Failed States

1. S. Sudan	9. Haiti
2. Somalia	10. Pakistan
3. CAR	11. Zimbabwe
4. DR Congo	12. Guinea
5. **Sudan**	13. **Iraq**
6. Chad	14. Côte d'Ivoire
7. Afghanistan	15. **Syria**
8. **Yemen**	

2014 Top 15 Defence Spending as % GDP

1. Afghanis.	14.6 %	9. DR Congo	5.1 %
2. **Oman**	12.0 %	10. Azerbaij.	4.5 %
3. **S. Arabia**	10.4 %	11. **Jordan**	4.3 %
4. S. Sudan	8.8 %	12. Armenia	4.3 %
5. **Iraq**	8.1 %	13. **Yemen**	4.2 %
6. **Israel**	7.6 %	14. **Bahrain**	3.9 %
7. **Algeria**	5.3 %	15. Myanmar	3.9 %
8. Angola	5.2 %		

2014 Proved Oil Reserves

■ N. America
■ S.&C. America
■ Eurasia
■ M. East
■ Africa
■ Asia

Sources: IISS, Fund of Peace, BP (excl. oil sands)

The Middle East remains one of the planet's major conflict arenas. It is among the highest military spenders. While global defence expenditures have been declining or only notching up slightly over the last three years, they have continued to grow by more than 10 % in the Middle East. Among the 15 countries with the highest defence expenditures in relations to GDP, more than half are from the Middle East.

Conversely, when we look at the Index of Failed States, put together annually by the Fund Peace, Middle East and African countries predominante. This may look paradoxical as some of these states simultaneously have high military expenditures. But the Index of Failed States indicates how well the state serves its citizens across the board with government services - schools, hospitals, infrastructure. In many Middle Eastern states, the military is the only state institutions that works. All the rest is either inexistent, or just barely existing.

If the Middle East were negligible to, say, the global economy, you could argue, from a cynical perspective, that the region's plight and drama matter little to outsiders. But apart from the humanitarian concerns we all should have for the poor human rights record and human tragedies that engulf the region, the Middle East is of course of particular geo-economic relevance. It holds half of the planet's proved oil reserves. The picture does not change much when we add tar sands in Canada and Venezuela. And the picture isn't too different either when we look at world gas reserves. Oil and gas remain in many respects the lubricants of the global economy, especially also in Asia, which has become the growth engine of the global economy regardless the current Chinese slowdown. Political risk thus hangs like a Damocles' Sword over the global supply of oil and gas.

Why is the Middle East so conflict-prone? What are the roots of all these wars, revolutions and instabilities?

I am a historian by training, so when trying to understand complex and complicated matters, I often refer to their historical genesis. This of course doesn't necessarily provide an answer how to deal with the situation going forward, or to forecast how things will develop in the future as there is ofen no such thing as linear continuity. Still, I find history usually a useful method to **understand**, as much as possible, what happened and what are the causes of what we see as effects today.

In many respects, what the Middle East is in today can be compared to a hundred year's war. And unfortunately, like the real Hundred Years' War between the kingdoms of France and England in the Middle Ages, this hundred years' war is likely to last for more than exactly a hundred years.

It is about 100 years ago that a cluster of event occurred that shaped the Middle East profoundly and initiated some of the continuities which are at play still today.

A century ago, much of what we call the Middle East today was still part of the Turkish Ottoman Empire. Egypt was a *de facto* British protectorate since 1882 though it was nominally still an Ottoman province. Also much of the southern rim of the Arabian peninsula and the sheikhdoms of the Persian Gulf were under British control. The inner parts of the Arabian peninsula were a collection of tribal confederations, with the house of Saud, the current rulers of the kingdom of Saudi Arabia, already in the ascent. Iran finally, or as it was called back then Persia, was nominally independent, but under pressure from both Tsarist Russia in the North and Britain in the East and South. For the British, the expansion into Arabia and Persia were part of their larger effort to secure and defend their Indian Empire.

The Hundred Year's War

- ## How it all began
  - 1907: Anglo-Russian division of Persia
  - 1909: Discovery of oil in Abadan
  - 1914: First World War
  - 1916: Sykes-Picot Agreement, Arab revolt in Hijaz
  - 1917: Balfour Declaration
  - 1921: Cairo conference: "Peace to end all peace" (David Fromkin)

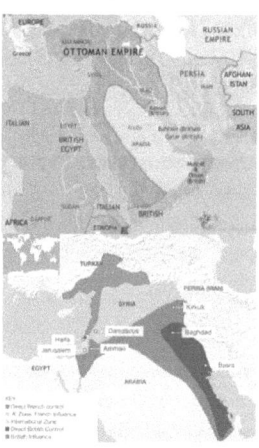

Source.: http://www.timemaps.com/history-middle-east-1914ad.
http://www.bbc.com/news/world-middle-east-25299553

In 1907 – so 108 years ago -, the British and the Russian formally divided Persia into zones of influence. And it was in the British zone of influence, near the city of Abadan, that oil was discovered in 1909 – 106 years ago. This was an important discovery as the Royal Navy, the most powerful navy back then, was just shifting from coal to oil firing. The discovery near Abadan allowed the Royal Navy greater autonomy in its oil supply. The discovery of oil also stands at the beginning of the region's role as the global oil reservoir.

In 1914 – 101 years ago -, the First World War broke out. It pitted the Central Powers, with Germany, Austria-Hungary, Bulgaria and the Ottoman Empire, against the Allies, i.e., France, Britan and Russia. In order to prevail against the Turks in the Middle East, the British instigated the Arab tribes to raise against their Ottoman rulers, making them to believe that after the war they would gain independence. Yet, behind the scenes, the British were already dividing up the loot with the French: Mr. Sykes and Monsieur Picot, a British and French diplomat, negotiated the respective agreement in 1916. You can see this on the bottom part of the map on this slide, with the greenish parts going to France and the greyish parts to Britain. This programmed a collision course between European colonial aspirations and the promise of independence to the Arabs.

But matters become even more complicated when the British also made promises to the World Jewish Congress one year later, i.e., 98 years ago. Secretary of State Arthur Balfour communicated to Lord Rothschild that the British government would view with favour the establishment of a national home for the Jewish people in what is Israel today, and that they would make necessary efforts to fulfil this idea. Another collision course was programmed.

3

Hence when the war ended, there was a mess to be sorted out. The Versailles Peace Conference divided the Middle East according to the Sykes-Picot agreement. This led to an Arab uprising in Syria in 1920. It was quelled by the French. Also the British had troubles with the Arab population in "their" area while riots broke out in Palestine against the promises to the World Jewish Congress. Eventually, the British convened a conference in Cairo to sort out the mess. The conference was successful inasmuch as it created the two countries of Iraq and Jordan and draw many of the boundaries in the region that are in place until today. But beyond this, the conference settled very little – in fact, it was a peace conference to end all peace in the region, as a British journalist turned historian, David Fromkin, had aptly termed it in a title to a book he published about the events.

Landmark events in the making of today's Middle East

- 1947/48: Foundation of Israel
- 1967: Six Day War
- 1979: Iranian Revolution/Camp David peace/Soviet invasion Afghanistan
- 1991: Gulf War
- 2001/03: 9/11 and Iraq invasion
- 2011: Arab Spring

Since then Middle Eastern history has developed through a set of landmark events which I have listed here. They formed to a large extent the Middle East we know today.

- 1947/48: The foundation of Israel. The Arab-Israeli conflict has remained ever since the original conflict to the region. Whatever separates Muslims and Arabs from each other in the region, they usually agree on Israel being their enemy number one, even if this commitment is only rhetorical. But as we are going to see in a minute, narratives are critical in the region.
- 1967: The Six Days War: It was a humiliating defeat for the Arabs and marked the demise of Arab nationalism while establishing Israel's military superiority over the region.

- 1979 – This was the year with three landmark events: The Iranian Revolution which saw for the first time political Islam entering centre stage; the Israeli-Egyptian peace treaty; and the Soviet invasion of Afghanistan, very much at the margins of what could be considered the Middle East, but still important as an influencing event when it comes to political Islam and what followed from 9/11 and al-Qaida.
- 1991: The Gulf War. This contained Saddam Hussein's expansionism in der region, but also massively enlarged the footprint of the US in the region.
- 2001/03: 9/11 and the subsequent invasion of Iraq. This meant the culmination point of the US power and influence in the region, but in the end produced such a mixed outcome that the US started to withdraw geopoltically and geoeconomically from the region with the termination of the Iraqi occupation in 2011.
- 2011: The Arab Spring. A very hopeful event in the beginning, but as we know by now it has plunged a number of countries into chaos and turmoil, such as Syria, Libya and Yemen, intermittently also Egypt, Tunisia and Bahrain.

Note: most of these events are somehow related to violence, to war, to atrocities. The sole exceptionis the Israeli-Egyptian peace of 1979 – and it has remained isolated as a "cold" peace in this regional arena of conflicts.

The conflict mindset

- Winner takes all
  - Compromise is weakness
- I against my brothers, my brothers and I against our cousins, my cousins and I against strangers
  - Hierarchy of loyalties
- The enemy of my enemy is my friend
  - Unholy alliances
- Conspiracies abound
  - The 10 percent of Coca Cola
  - Who's in bed with whom

The bloody trajectory of events has fostered a certain mindset and conflict culture that permeates the whole region. I would like to highlight some aspects of this here.

First, there is a wide-spread "Winner takes all" mentality. Only total victory is acceptable, nothing else (which of course then also means total defeat for the adversary). Compromise is seen as weakness and has no value; if there is compromise, parties involved look out for the next opportunity to overturn it and make it a total victory.

Secondly, there is permanent struggle across concentric circles of loyalties. The bedouin proverb "I against my brothers, my brothers and I against our cousins, my cousins, my brothers and I against strangers" encapsulates this finely. Most Arabs and Muslims are hostile to Israel. But then they break up into factions fighting each other, and in practice do much more of that than fighting Israel: secularists against Islamists, Shi'ite Islamists against Sunni Islamists, Wahhabi/Salafi Sunni Islamists against Brotherhood Sunni Islamists, in Syria now the radical Sunni Islamists of the al Qaida-allied Nusra Front against the radical Sunni Islamists of the Islamic State, and so on.

Third, the permanence of these struggles also leads to a permanent need for alliances as most groups are too weak to prevail on their adversaries with their own forces only. Alliances are closed by sheer necessity, after the pseudo-mathematical formula of "The enemy of my enemy is my friend." There is mostly little regard for the narratives involved or the ideology held by the presumptive ally. Unholy alliances are legion in the Middle East. Just to take a current example: the nominally Socialist, nominally secular Assad regime is allied with avowedly Islamist Iran and the Lebanese Shi'ite Hizbullah. Their opponents, the Syrian rebels, are now for the most part Islamists, so in principle sharing the same vision of an Islamic state and society, though the Sunni variety of it. But in reality they are at each other's throat. Iran and Hizbullah, on the other hand, are the protectors of Syria's many non-Muslim minorities as these tend to side with the Assad regime.

An important point needs to be added, however. Because these alliances are unholy, they for the most part of short-lived and only tactical, until they have exhausted their utility. Alliances are shifting permanently. And there is no moral onus for reneging on an alliance promise. Rather, it is seen as tactically savvy.

And this then plays into the next feature I would like to mention: the Middle East is fertile ground for conspiracy theories. Nothing too absurd not to be believed. One story, for instance, has it that Coca Cola transfers each year 10 percent of its annual profit to Israel. No rationale why they should do so. But it is believed. OK, this may be at the outer rim of the crazy stories. There are more plausible narratives going around, at least being more plausible at first sight. But they often lose their credibility and plausibility as well at second sight. Conspiracy theories are mostly craftfully constructed around who is in bed with whom and why: On the last point, the answer is almost mechanistically attributed to oil, even in countries where there is no oil. Because these stories are constantly repeated, they are eventually believed even when there is no factual base for them. These stories poison the overall climate in the region, undermine trust, foreclose political options and support the throwback to one's own community.

This conflict mindset has a profound impact on state and politics in the region – mostly on Arab states, on Iran, but to a much lesser extent also on Israel and Turkey (Turkey effectively was not much of a Middle Eastern state until recently). It has shaped the structure of political power and decision-making in a particular way which I would like to briefly elaborate here.

Politics and state in the Middle East

- Visible and invisible power structures
  - Insiders and outsiders
- Decision-making behind the curtain
  - The guy behind the guy behind the guy
- Narratives are critical
  - Legitimising function
- Need for external patrons
  - US, Russia, others – weapons, technology
  - Regional sponsors: e.g., Iraq
- The impotent macho state paradox: appearing strong while being weak

The state in the Middle East normally has a dual power structure. What do I mean with this? As other states, Middle Eastern states have a president or a king, a parliament, a constitution, possibly a supreme court and so on. This is what I call the visible power structure. But they also have an invisible power structure – the real allocation of power – and invariably this is the more important structure. To some extent, this is of course true for many other countries, even for transparent democracies sometimes. But in the Middle East, this phenomenon is particularly pronounced. You don't get what you see.

Political power, and with this economic power and any other sort of power, is usually held by a small group of people related to each other by ethnic, sectarian, religious, regional or family commonalities. They hold such power exclusively, i.e., they are the insiders. Outsiders to this group have not access to any positions of real power.

Yet, even the small groups holding power are further split into factions which are constantly fighting each other over control of state resources. Even under pressure from the outside, such fighting often does not stop. Just to give you an example: When Iraq had already lost the Gulf War against the US-led coalition and was under heavy sanctions in the early 1990s, fighting within the extended Saddam Hussein family was so much entrenched and ritualised that it continued unabated. Very often this meant that actually blood was spilt. So, for instance, Saddam's rogue son Uday shot his half-uncle Watban Ibrahim during a dispute so heavily, that Ibrahim's leg had to be amputated and allegedly also his genitals. Ibrahim was not a Nobody in the regime. Saddam had entrusted him with important security jobs. Some time later, Uday was shot in an ambush and while he largely recovered from his wounds, he remained partially handicapped for the short rest of his life (he was shot in 2003 by US forces). There was agreement that this ambush was a revenge attack by other regime insiders who had suffered from Uday's bloodthirsty unpredictabilities.

Now imagine, these guys being besieged in the drab Baghdad of the 1990s, with all incentives in place to hang together as much as possible in order to avoid hanging separately. But they had nothing better to do than to go after each other, as much as they went after anybody else. Maybe the Saddam Husseins were an especially despicable and rotten bunch, hardly different what you know from the worst American mafia movies. Still, it is amazing.

The fact that power is held within a tightly knit group that is permanently at each other's throat also explains why decision-making is often so blurred, complicated and endless in the region. As a foreigner and outside, you never know whether the guy you are dealing with is really the guy who can make decisions that matter, or whether there is another guy behind him who really pulls the strings – or whether there is even a third guy behind both of them.

All this feeds into the next point, namely the criticality of narratives. I mentioned the perseverance of conspiracy theories in the Middle East. The importance of narratives is the one element we Westerners often have most difficulties to understand when dealing with the region – why can't these Middle Easterners do away with permanently accusing each other of being in bed with, say, Israel or the US while in practice many of them are dealing with either or both countries anyway? Why can't they simply be candid and admit that publicly? But in an environment where a conflict mindset prevails, this is impossible. By admitting being in bed with Israel or the US, you are only strengthening the narrative of your enemies against you. Narratives justify why the region is in a constant conflict mode and why there can be no solution without the total defeat of adversaries and enemies.

Sometimes, it is said that the Middle Eastern leaders use the narratives only for public consumption while in private they are pragmatic and even deride these narratives. There may be cases where this is so. On the other hand, there is consistent evidence that Arab leaders privately believe what they preach publicly, from a balcony and in front of agitated masses. For instance, to quote the Iraqi example again, there are many hours of tape-recorded private conversations of Saddam Hussein with his aides – so not with strangers and foreigners whom he told what they liked to hear – where he essentially reiterated in private what he said in public. And accordingly was his decision-making.

The weakness and brittleness of the states carved out of the Ottoman Empire in the 1920s, and the fact that the regime subsequently installed all relied initially on colonial powers made external patrons for the regimes a fact of life early on. That the influence of such external powers has remained and continued to this day has many reasons – oil, ideology, the need for weapons and technology. Although being a region of conflict, the Middle East has never developed an armament industry of any noteworthy capability. Consequently, weapons had to be imported from the outside in order to actually fight out the conflicts. Saudi Arabia today is the world's largest weapons' importer. This explains why the US, but also Russia, France and other powers are still having a big say in the region. Moreover, regimes in the region see an external patron as indispensable although it could be argued that in most of the cases a patron simultaneously weakens the regimes in the eyes of their own population. In this, the regimes fall into the trap of their own narratives which hold that the Middle East is an area of competing great powers where you can survive only by allying with an external patron. Israel with its strong alliance with the US, serves as a paragon here.

Yet, the phenomenon of foreign influence isn't limited to external powers only. Also Middle Eastern states are constantly meddling into each other affairs, sponsoring local proxies. Almost all Middle Eastern governments are engaging in this "game", and you can take almost any conflict in the region to discern the hand of neighbours behind the different conflict parties. Take the example of Iraq again: today, the Shi'ites are relying on Iran, the Kurds on the Turks (at least partly), and the Sunnis have had on and off support from the Saudis.

All this leads to what I would call the impotent macho state paradox. Middle Eastern regimes often look strong, with their armies and their well developed security apparatuses. But in reality they are often weak. The social base of the regimes is small and fractious, the political legitimacy of the rulers is brittle and hollow, and this effectively makes the regimes, and with them the states they "possess", weak. Look at Yemen today – as we have seen, it has one of the highest military expenditures, but it is close to state collapse. Mubarak, the former president for 30 years, looked so strong und untouchable. He was ousted within a fortnight.

Against this background, let's now trace the development of the one phenomenon that has captured most of the headlines about the Middle East over the last, say, 1 ½ years, namely the emergence and establishment of ISIS, or the Islamic State as it calls itself now. Much has been written on paper and online about ISIS. And in all candour: quite a bit of this is utter rubbish. Too often, Western media blindly believe another variety of Middle Eastern conspiracy theories.

The roots and origins of ISIS go effectively back to the late 1980s and are closely associated with one man, a Palestinian Jordanian named Ahmad Fadeel al-Nazal al-Khalayleh. He later adopted the *nom de guerre* Abu Musab al-Zarqawi under which he gained notoriety. He was born in 1966 to a poor family in the north of the country. One has to add here that Palestinians, i.e., Arabs who fled after the foundation of Israel, make up more than half of the Jordanian population. However, power in Jordan is held by the so-called Transjordanians, i.e., the descendents of the tribes who inhabited the desert east of the Jordan river when the country was established in the first place. So Zarqawi, to go by the point I made about power structures in the Middle East, was born into the outsider community of Jordan. I don't want to read too much into this fact – there are millions of young Jordanians born into the outsider community, and they do not turn into terrorists. Still, it is noteworthy that the ultimate founder of ISIS came from an outsider background.

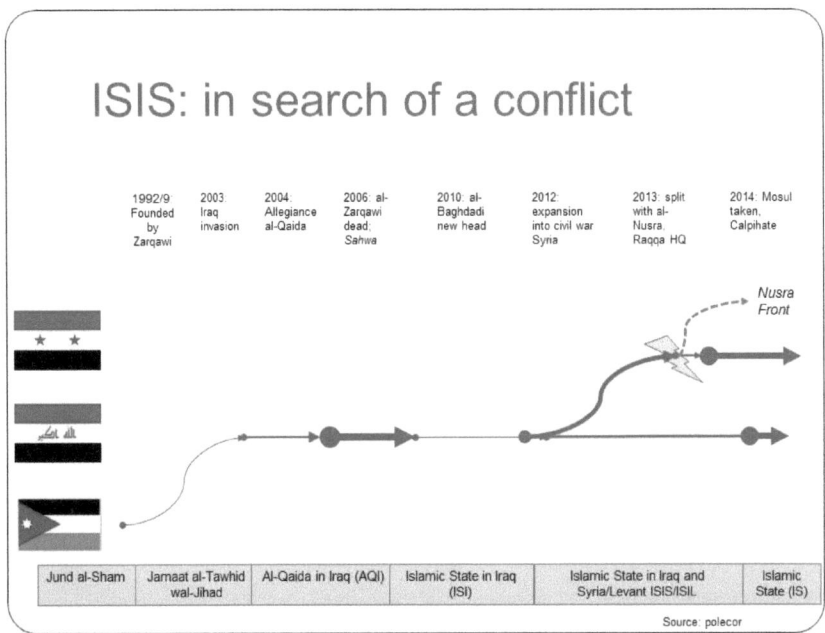

ISIS: in search of a conflict

1992/9	2003:	2004:	2006: al-	2010: al-	2012:	2013: split	2014: Mosul
Founded	Iraq	Allegiance	Zarqawi	Baghdadi	expansion	with al-	taken,
by	invasion	al-Qaida	dead;	new head	into civil war	Nusra,	Caliphate
Zarqawi			Sahwa		Syria	Raqqa HQ	

Nusra Front

Jund al-Sham	Jamaat al-Tawhid wal-Jihad	Al-Qaida in Iraq (AQI)	Islamic State in Iraq (ISI)	Islamic State in Iraq and Syria/Levant ISIS/ISIL	Islamic State (IS)

Source: polecor

As a young man, Zarqawi travelled to Afghanistan. Apparently, he planned to fight the Soviets, but he ended up being a reporter instead. He met Osama bin Laden and, probably more important, also Abdullah Azzam, a radical Palestinian preacher who formed much of the jihadi ideology of al-Qaida.

Returned to Jordan, Zarqawi helped setting up an organisation that give itself the name Jund al-Sham, which means something like "Military Garrison of al-Sham". The term al-Sham is an interesting one as ISIS is using it as well – the second S in the English acronym of ISIS stands for al-Sham. It denotes a particular geography which is not congruent with today's borders and includes an area that basically covers Israel, Jordan, Lebanon, Western Syria and the Turkish province of Hatay. This is the reason why sometimes al-Sham is translated into English with the term "Levant" (and hence the acronym ISIL in English), but Levant actually covers a much wider area than al-Sham. Anyway, cut a long story short: using the term al-Sham in the nomination of a political group like Jund al-Sham or ISIS can be read as a shorthand political statement for "We do not recognise existing borders". Which is already a pretty revolutionary programme in itself.

Jund-al Sham was quickly crushed by the Jordanian security services. Zarqawi was arrested and sent to prison where he radicalised further. After his release, he founded another organisation in 1999, called Jamaat al-Tawhid wal Jihad which roughly translates as "Society for Unity and Holy War". Again, using Tawhid in the group's name comes close to a political statement. Theologically, Tawhid denotes the unity of God, i.e., there is only one God and that God is only one. Radical Sunnis sometimes accuse Shi'ites of violating this unity because they venerate Ali, the cousin and son-in-law of Muhammad the Prophet, and the imams, i.e., the descedents of Ali. In the eyes of radical Sunnis, the cult around Ali and the imams amounts to polytheism, and thus apostasy from Islam –which according to the Sharia is punished by death. In practice, using the term Tawhid amounts to a strongly anti-Shi'ite agenda.

Jamaat al-Tawhid wal Jihad was apparently mostly recruited among Palestinian Jordanians. Again, as Jund al-Sham, it was not very successful but it launched some terrorist attacks; meanwhile, Zarqawi was travelling through Iran and Iraq. It seems that he ended up in Baghdad when the US invaded Iraq. He now saw a big opportunity to launch a jihadi war in Iraq.

The ground was fertile. The downfall of the Saddam Hussein regime meant that the Arab Sunnis who had been the dominant and privileged ethnic and sectarian group under his rule lost their status at the expense of the Kurds and, more importantly, the majority Arab Shi'ites. In exploiting the grievances of the Arab Sunnis, Zarqawi expected to carry his Islamist agenda forward. But there were dozens, hundreds of Arab Sunni resistance groups in these heady days of 2003, so Zarqawi had to look for a unique selling point to strengthen his position.

He found it by doing two things: first, he proclaimed his allegiance to al-Qaida, and this allegiance was accepted by the al-Qaida leadership. The gesture boosted Zarqawi's credentials among Arab Sunni resistance groups, and Zarqawi renamed his group Al-Qaida in Iraq (AQI). At the same time, he advocated next to a terrorist campaign against the US occupation forces, a radically anti-Shi'ite agenda. Initially, Zarqawi was not without success. But he soon ran into trouble. The al-Qaida leadership was uneasy with Zarqawi's visceral hatred of Shi'ites. Though al-Qaida is also radically Sunni, its leadership argued that the focus of the struggle should be on fighting the Americans, and not the Shi'ites. It was rather embarrassing for a group like al-Qaida which so much preached an epic Pan-Islamic struggle against the US that its self-proclaimed foot soldiers in Iraq were busy killing fellow Muslims. Bin Laden and other al-Qaida leaders first privately and later publicly reprimanded Zarqawi for his anti-Shi'ite fervour and demanded a change of course.

Zarqawi's brutalities were not limited to Americans and Shi'ites. He also meted out cruel punishments against Arab Sunnis who did not agree with him. This made AQI rapidly losing support. Zarqawi was finally killed by US commandos in June 2006 and his group was rapidly reduced to a rump of several hundred fighters who survived at the margins of the Arab Sunni community.

AQI renamed itself Islamic State of Iraq (ISI). By now, both its leadership and rank and file were mostly Iraqi, with the Jordanians of the first hour either killed, detained or returned home. But there also was a small core of international Islamic fighters, coming from a wide array of different countries.

In the years after 2007/08, Iraq underwent a degree of stabilisation. Arab Sunnis continued to hold grievances, but made a serious effort to integrate into the new Iraq. Yet, this proved almost impossible, with hardline Shi'ite Prime Minister Maliki developing his own clientelistic, sectarian and authoritarian regime. After 2011, not least under the impact of events from the Arab Spring, the Sunnis began to claim their rights more vocally in peaceful protests. The Maliki government reacted with violence and repression.

Within ISI, a change of leadership occurred. In 2010, Muhammad al-Badri al-Samarai took over, also known under his *nom de guerre* Abu Bakr al-Baghdadi. He was an Iraqi with a degree in Islamic studies and had been active in the resistance since 2003. He had more ambitious plans than to simply hibernate his movement. He wanted to reach out beyond Iraq, turning ISI into a truly Pan-Sunni and international force. He purged the ISI leadership of opponents and resorted to more daring military actions, such as the mass liberation of prisoners from Iraqi jails. He also re-adopted Zarqawi's radical anti-Shi'ite rhetoric and sought alliances with other groups, including the remnants of Saddam Hussein's Baath party. As Arab Sunni grievances in Iraq mounted again, al-Baghdadi gradually gained in sympathy and support.

The situation in Syria gave him an opportunity to satisfy his cross-border ambitions. What had started as wide-spread popular protests across communities against the dictatorial regime of Assad family rapidly degenerated into a nasty sectarian civil war, pitching the Alawi community – a heterodox branch of Shi'ism – and other Syrian minorities against the majority of Arab Sunnis. In late 2011, al-Baghdadi sent Syrian members of ISI, money and weapons to Syria. They formed their own organisation – the Nusra Front – and took up the fighting along Arab Sunni rebels, adding important military knowledge. Initially, al-Baghdadi kept a low profile, and al-Nusra proved to be successful and popular. But when the self-confidence of al-Nusra soared, al-Baghdadi proclaimed the merger of al-Nusra with his ISI to the Islamic State of Iraq and al-Sham (ISIS). This did not go down with many Syrian al-Nusra fighters, and they split from ISIS, retaining both their name and allegiance to al-Qaida. The latter also heavily criticised al-Baghdadi who then as a consequence cut all links with al-Qaida. He declared that from now on the focus of the struggle in Syria should be on erecting an Islamic state, and not on the defeat of Assad. The provincial city of Raqqa became the main basis of ISIS in Syria.

Shortly after this, ISIS also moved with force into northern Iraq. The Iraqi army – trained, equipped and financed by the US and numerically superior to the ISIS force – simply collapsed within a matter of days. Mosul, Iraq's second largest city, fell into the hands of ISIS. Al-Baghdadi proclaimed himself the new Caliph. This moved him into the centre of extremist Islam world-wide, and thousands of radicalised volunteers began to flock to ISIS. Taking up the mantle of caliph was a smart move. With this, al-Baghdadi at least superficially appealed to the longing many Arab Sunnis have for the restoration of the Caliphate, i.e., a unified religious leadership of (Sunni) Muslims which had been abolished in 1924. However rash and illegitimate his move was among the vast majority of Muslims, he nonetheless impressed many with the step. And proclaiming a Caliphate, ISIS gained a critical edge over al-Qaida in the rivalry of extremist ideology leadership – Osama bin Laden, whatever his "merits" from an extremist standpoint, had never gotten to this point.

Summarising, ISIS ascent over the years bears testimony to our earlier finding that exclusivism is at the heart of violent clash in the region. It gained the upper hand because

Arab Sunnis had been excluded from power in Syria and Iraq – in the first case for more than three decades (while forming the majority of Syria's population), in the latter case since 2003. ISIS ascent also shows the importance of the narratives, as I just pointed out with the alleged restoration of the Caliphate. And the implosion of the macho state was clearly visible with the collapse of the Iraqi Army before Mosul.

Conspiracy theories, urban legends and outrageous stories have accompanied the rises and falls of ISIS in its different incarnations. I don't have the time to revisit them here. Just one I would like to discuss a bit more in detail as it is so often heard and repeated in the media.

And that is that ISIS is allegedly a US creation. I think I showed with my detailed account of ISIS' genesis that this certainly is not the case. ISIS, in its earlier incarnation of AQI, was always at the core of resistance against the US in Iraq, and ISIS has also undermined US efforts in Syria to form a coherent, moderate opposition front against Assad. But is the US totally clear of "guilt", if we use that heavy term? Well, the US has certainly made mistakes – a number of mistakes, you could argue. If I had to pinpoint the most serious one, my candidate would probably be the ill-advised policies the US followed in Iraq after the occupation. It had two major flaws: it was too reliant on a rather naïve belief in transferring democracy to a country like Iraq and it was too much focused on promoting sectarian and ethnic policies, splitting the Iraqi body politic from the beginning into the three constituencies of Arab Sunnis, Arab Shi'ites and Kurds, actually reinforcing the policies already pursued by Saddam Hussein instead of undoing them. Yet, it is always easy to criticise after the facts. And with hindsight, we are always smarter. If the "original sin" was the invasion of Iraq in 2003 – undoubtedly a "war of choice" -, then we have to admit that one alternative outcome to the invasion would be an Iraq today still ruled by Saddam Hussein and his rogue clique. A better solution? Ask the Iraqis.

But let's leave the speculation aside and return to ISIS. The fall of Mosul, the proclamation of the Caliphate and subsequent events, such as the despicable atrocities committed by ISIS against minorities and prisoners, have eventually galvanised the international community into action. An alliance was put together that united almost everybody: the US and the majority of Western governments, the government of Iraq, the Saudis and their GCC allies, the Kurds and Turkey, though the latter joined rather reluctantly and under a lot of pressure from Washington. Even Assad, though officially not a member of the coalition, objectively belongs to it.

And this coalition set in train the decline of ISIS. Since the taking of Mosul, it has suffered only reverses. I am convinced we have passed the inflection point in the group's trajectory. This is not to say that ISIS still has a number of strengths: they have been rather effective administrators of the territory under their rule, and their fighting force is still highly motivated, though reports are growing they have difficulties recruiting new fighters. Plus, ISIS continues to be a beacon for extremist Islamists. Radical groups in Nigeria, Libya and elsewhere have plaid allegiance to the Caliphate as erected by ISIS.

The demise of ISIS: the way to go

- International coalition after Mosul
- Strengths of ISIS
  - Well-organised territory
  - Highly motivated fighting force
  - Continued attractiveness to extremist fringe
- Weaknesses of ISIS
  - Coalition works
  - Very little popular support, and further dwindling
  - Declining economic assets
  - Declining military assets
- Redoubt in Syria

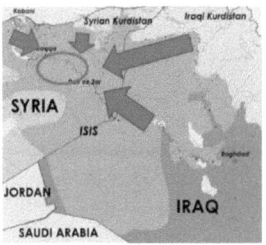

Source: http://arsenalfordemocracy.com/2015/02/05/jordan-to-re-enter-the-isis-war-now-in-iraq/western-iraq-eastern-syria-isis-map-jordan-saudi-arabia-february-3-2015/

But there are also a number of weaknesses, and they will eventually prevail as they become stronger by the day. First and foremost, there is the coalition which I mentioned. It has remained solid and effective in spite of the many differences that separate their members from each other. And it is likely to remain so for another while. Then there is, in the end, little genuine popular support for ISIS in the region it governs – more in Iraq than in Syria, true. But the brutalities ISIS extended also on Arab Sunnis when they did not tow the ISIS line has undermined the little support that was there in the beginning. And it will further erode as ISIS is contained and pushed back. Furthermore, ISIS' economic assets and resources are dwindling. In 2013 and 2014, they had made quite some money with oil smuggling from Syria's eastern oil fields into Turkey. But many of these installations have now be destroyed by air raids, Turkey has closed its borders, and the decline in oil prices has also left a gap in ISIS' coffers. And last but not least, ISIS military assets are deteriorating. When ISIS took Mosul, they captured large stocks of US equipment belonging to the Iraqi Army. Much of this equipment has now been destroyed, or is degrading due to a lack of maintenance and spare parts. Ammunition supplies are exhausted, and ISIS has increasingly to rely on purchases from corrupt Iraqi and Syrian officers – not really a reliable supply line.

All this sums up to forcing ISIS into retreat. As the current fighting around Tikrit in Iraq suggests, resistance is still strong. But retreat could turn into a rout at some point, and this tipping point may possibly be rather closer than further.

Will ISIS disappear? Probably not entirely. I expect the international coalition to become less cohesive at one point when the immediate danger posed by ISIS has receded. This will translate into less pressure on ISIS. It may well hold out in a redoubt in eastern Syria, as it held out in the Arab Sunni parts of Iraq after 2006. But by then, it will have become a rather marginal player, one of the many armed groups that we have in Syria today and possibly eventually blending in with one of them.

What's after ISIS?

- Iraq
  - Sunni Arabs marginalised
  - Iran as the predominant power
- Iran
  - Builds its hegemony further, nuclear deal with P5+1
- Kurds
- Syria
  - Tilting towards Assad…
- Israel
  - Suspicious of Iran
- US
  - Withdrawal from the region continues, pivoting towards Asia

---

Which brings us to the question: What will happen after the demise of ISIS? What will the region look like?

Of course, there is a lot of room for speculation on this. But I will still indicate some contours that are already recognisable.

In Iraq, the losers will be the Arab Sunnis. Notwithstanding the vows of the Iraqi government to become more inclusive and to avoid repeating the mistakes committed after 2006, I do not foresee the Arab Sunnis playing a major role any more – as a community. (It may be different with individuals). They will have to accept that going forward they will be a minority – and a small one for that. Dreams of restoring their ascendancy as they enjoyed under Saddam Hussein are just pipedreams. They will also suffer economically, as their region has been ravaged by war and insurgency for now more than 10 years. They will be poor, disenfranchised and disillusioned.

Conversely, the winners will be the Shi'ites who will see their ascendancy confirmed, and the big winner will also be Iran which is likely to become the most influential foreign power in the country. This is not to say that all Iraqi Shi'ites are happy about this Iranian predominance, and the Shi'ites themselves are far from being an unified bloc. But for the time being, a direct clash between Iran and the Shi'ites in Iraq is unlikely.

Iran will also benefit from an upcoming agreement with the P5+1 over its nuclear programme. Meanwhile, Iran now has significant political influence in Baghdad, Beirut and – with current events in Yemen – may also solidify such influence in Sanaa. Saudi Arabia, on the other hand, will see this as a set-back for its own policies. The Saudi-Iranian competition is likely to continue.

More difficult to estimate is what will happen with the Kurds. They of course provided the bulk of fighters in those difficult days when ISIS took Mosul. And the Kurds also inflicted, together with the allied air force, the first real military reverse on ISIS in Kobane. But the Kurds are divided among themselves, and their dream of their own state is as far removed from realisation as ever. Their fate will eventually play out in the national policy framework of the individual states – Iraq, Turkey, Syria and Iran. And the governments in these four countries, or the groups claiming for themselves the right to represent the government, may hate each other: where they all agree is that their borders should be inviolable and that Kurdish separatism must be contained.

Also in Syria, an assessment is difficult. Who benefits from the demise of ISIS? Assad or the opposition? Within the opposition, the al-Nusra front now seems to be the most powerful group. But al-Nusra remains faithful to al-Qaida, and this disqualifies it –and with it an increasing share of the Syrian opposition – for the US. So in the end, Assad may benefit more than the opposition. The US recently indicated that it may resume talks with him about a political settlement. Such a settlement is a chimera for the time being. But the simple fact that the US is willing to talk to Assad again amounts to a rehabilitation. And is likely to lead to further acrimony between the US and the Saudis who continue to stick to the anti-Assad agenda.

Let's briefly look at Israel as well. It has not been much directly involved with this whole ISIS story, though it has been of course a keen observer from the sidelines. Israel is mostly concerned about the ascendancy of Iran. But there is some disagreement within the country how to deal with the challenge. The just re-elected Prime Minister Binyamin Netanyahu advocates a robust and active policy. I think he would even consider allying with countries like Saudi Arabia to contain Iran, as it is already the case with Egypt with which Israel cooperates against Hamas, the Muslim Brotherhood and extremist terrorists in the Sinai. But openly allying with Israel remains difficult for most Arab governments. Israel's military and security establishment is more hesitant than Netanyahu and while worried about Iran as well it rather favours even closer coordination and alignment with the US. As for the nuclear component in this equation, Israel is of course vastly superior, making deterrence vis-à-vis Israel a credible and long-term option.

And finally the US. The pushback of ISIS will allow the US to continue its strategic extraction from Middle East that has begun in 2011. Of course, the US will remain an important external player in the region, not least as the core tenet of the commitment to the Middle East – America's security guarantee for Israel – will not wane. But all the other elements that bound the US to region have been moving over the last years. The US is increasingly focusing its strategic resources on what President Obama has called the 'Asian pivot'- translating into managing and checking China's ascent to the status of a new great power. The return of American advisers and military planes to Iraq to wage war on ISIS has not reversed this basic strategic trend, and an end of the campaign against ISIS will further accelerate it.

With this in mind, one may argue that the demise of ISIS means largely a return to the *status quo ante*, though with some important nuances. I would agree with this sombre assessment. The Middle East will not become a more peaceful, more stable or more prosperous place once the evil of ISIS is removed.

The end of the Hundred Years' War?

- **The Middle East's Jeanne d'Arc in sight?**
- **Big hope of Arab spring dashed**
- **Perseverance of the conflict mind**
- **New great power rivalries**
- **Comfort from Asia and Latin America**

Which brings me full circle to my opening statement about the Hundred Year's War in the Middle East. Is there no Joan of Arc in sight to end the turmoil in the region? Unfortunately, the answer is no.

The Arab spring with its claims for democracy, human rights and accountability seemed to offer a glimpse of hope a couple of years ago. But in the end it turned out making things worse. The conflict mindset has persevered and in many respects even intensified. The Arab Spring has also fuelled the rivalry between Iran and Saudi Arabia. The US withdrawal from the region showed that the conflicts and confrontations in the Middle East – contrary to what many claim – are not imported, but home-made. The US withdrawal will leave a power vaccuum in some respects, but it may be filled again with new great power rivalries in the somewhat distant future, such as between China and India who both have become major oil importers from the region.

So is there really nothing going to change? Are we condemned to see the Middle East trapped –almost infinitely? – in war, bloodshed and atrocities? Will there ever be an end game to all that?

I don't have a crystal ball. We can only draw hope from historical analogies. Other regions in the past were arenas of permanent conflict, often for decades – just remember East and Southeast Asia a few decades ago. China was embroiled in war and revolution for more than a 100 years, starting with the Opium War and ending with the Cultural Revolution. Today, it has become one of the engines of the global economy. I am not saying that the Middle East will become a geo-economic engine. But what we can derive from the example is that conflicts do end at one point. This gives us hope. Yet, when, where, how this will be in the case of the Middle East – we don't know.

Bibliography:

Internet sources:

http://fsi.fundforpeace.org/

http://www.bp.com/content/dam/bp/pdf/Energy-economics/statistical-review-2014/BP-statistical-review-of-world-energy-2014-full-report.pdf

Print sources:

David Fromkin, A peace to end all peace. Creating the modern Middle East, 1914-1922. London, 1989

Gary Gambill. "Abu Musab Al-Zarqawi: A Biographical Sketch". Terrorism Monitor, vol 2, issue 24, 2007

Ahmed S. Hashim. Iraq's Sunni Insurgency. Adelphi Paper 402. Oxon, 2009

International Institute of Strategic Studies. The Military Balance 2013-2015. London, 2013-2015

Volker Perthes, Geheime Gärten. Die neue arabische Welt. O.O. o.J.

Andrew Phillips, "How al Qaeda lost Iraq. Australian Journal of International Affairs, vol. 63, no. 1, 2009, pp. 64-84

Rolf Tanner, "Conflict and narrative in the Middle East". Survival, vol. 56, no. 2, 2014, pp. 89-108